A CHAPLET
OF ROSES

A CHAPLET
OF ROSES

Twenty-four Poems
by
MICHAEL MURPHY

TOGA

First published by Toga Books
Dublin, Ireland
www.michaelmurphyauthor.com

Copyright © 2015 Michael Murphy

Paperback	ISBN: 978-1-911013-04-4
Ebook – mobi format	ISBN: 978-1-911013-05-1
Ebook – ePub format	ISBN: 978-1-911013-06-8
CreateSpace	ISBN: 978-1-911013-07-5

A CIP catalogue record for this book is
available from the British Library

Produced by Kazoo Independent Publishing Services
222 Beech Park, Lucan, Co. Dublin
www.kazoopublishing.com

Kazoo Independent Publishing Services is not the publisher of this work. All rights and responsibilities pertaining to this work remain with Toga Books.

Kazoo offers independent authors a full range of publishing services.
For further details visit www.kazoopublishing.com

Cover design by Andrew Brown
Printed in the EU

My mother died this year in May. Shortly afterwards, I dreamed that my brother Kieran, who had died some twenty years before, was giving me a big grin from outside his bedroom door in the family home on the Mall in Castlebar. He said that Mum was about to arrive.

"Where is she going to sleep?" I asked.

And he said, "She'll sleep in here," showing me the back room, the store room for her wool shop. It was the first bedroom I had as a child, equipped with a comforting night-light, a star shining above in the firmament just for me.

*A Chaplet of Rose*s is my prayer to her.

Contents

Some Personal Poems ...

The Mayo Sequence ...

Foreword
Dr Jeannine Woods

A CHAPLET OF ROSES IS a wreath of roses worn on the head, and also a rosary or string of beads used in counting prayers. It developed as a figurative sense from the original meaning of *rosarie*, or rose garden, conveying the idea of a "garden" of prayers. The poems in Michael Murphy's second collection of poetry are indeed beautifully contemplative. Each is a rose expressing love for his partner, for friends, for nature and animals and humankind. I also consider them to be true prayers, even though Michael writes "I feel bereft of God ..." He continues in that particular poem, "Bereft", with an advanced interpretation of Christianity, emphasising a religious reality which is constructed out of language: "At least I have the language still/To express impossible truths and capture the ineffable/To underpin my life with meaningful myths/The birth of immanence/The crucifixion of truth/The resurrection of hope/ And perhaps that final stage of growing up/The ascension to mature human responsibility/Without the joyful presence of my God/With all the sharp-eyed clarity of a Presbyterian elder." All of the poems in this heartfelt collection continue this poet's exploration of a reality which is created out of language. They are informed by the three strands of Michael Murphy's career as broadcaster, psychoanalyst and author, and make for a deeply satisfying, rich and emotional engagement, featuring poems which reach out to touch the heart and appeal to the intellect.

There is an unremitting emphasis on the significance of love throughout this collection. In the poem "Enough", which he wrote for a friend who was dying, he concludes "Love was all that mattered/In the end ..." The opening poem, "And When You Speak of Trees" states that "... love is the firmest groundwork of our being/With roots to anchor truth ..." In the poem "Bad Behaviour Can Get Elephants Killed", he says that "Animals do not belong to us/They allow us to live near them/To be graced by their honour/To learn from their integrity/To encourage gentleness/And lay hold of tenderness/To allow ourselves to love them/And be loved a hundredfold in return ..." And in the poem "I Shall Die", the poet first describes himself in humble terms, and then after having undergone the transfiguring power of love, he is repositioned: "I was an unimportant person ... Nevertheless I was loved once/By someone special/And I loved him in return/We glimpsed eternity together ..."

For the first time, Michael employs his poetic gifts to examine his Irish heritage in a sequence of poems which speaks lovingly of his home in Castlebar, County Mayo. "Home To Mayo" is an anthem, the verses of which are designed to be sung or chanted in alternate parts. In this long and important poem, there is an unassuming line which captures the essence of this poet who feels misplaced, and gives us an explanation of the type of person we are dealing with: "In my mind I always live at home in Mayo ..." He says, "I am the resurrection welling up/From successive imprints on my soul/They have written their names on my body/Like the ancient ogham inscriptions on the standing stones/Of Erris and Murrisk and Costello ..." This linguistic imprinting on his soul and writing on his body from his Mayo ancestors have made Michael who he is. "My ancient roots are silently asleep/Beneath the brown blanket bog of Ballycroy

..." And he says "Today it is my turn to give them voice/To make known in my living all of their untold stories/For the West is awake in me ..." The centrality of place in imagining history, identity and community figures large in Irish tradition and in contemporary literature, notably in the poetry of Seamus Heaney and the dramatic works of Brian Friel. "Home to Mayo" builds on this tradition and on the theme of exile. There is longing in the lines "Mostly I miss the warm embrace of the Mayo accent/That kiss on the lips blowing in off the Atlantic with the sea spray/Soft and fierce and salty easy ..." And he continues "Mayo talk is a baptism that strengthens my spirit/ It fills me with hope and immerses me in certainty ..." Three times he returns to the supplicatory refrain "These are my people/This is my place" as if to underline and emphasise to those capable of hearing and understanding the necessity of that truth. In his work on language and landscape among the Western Apache, anthropologist Keith Basso points out that landscapes are not solely part of the material universe: "landscapes are always available to their seasoned inhabitants in other than material terms. Landscapes are available in symbolic terms as well, and so, chiefly through the manifold agencies of speech ... landscapes and the places that fill them become tools for the imagination ... eminently portable possessions to which individuals can maintain deep and abiding attachments, regardless of where they travel". The Mayo Sequence of poems illustrates the truth that those landscapes which we inhabit also inhabit us, and celebrates the imaginative possibilities of that co-(in)-habitation.

The importance of the truth is a theme running throughout the collection, and is explained in "Home to Mayo" in terms of the poet's ancestry. Recalling 1798, and "those faithful Mayo patriots/ Who fought for their freedom at the Races of Castlebar/First citizen President John Moore's republic/Founded on being free to tell the whole truth without fear ...", he says, "We owe them the freedom to speak in the fullness of truth/To let each Mayoman have his say without fear in this republic ..." Immediately he takes centre-stage in the poem by pointing out for the third time: "I am a Mayo man, born and bred/I have the character of a Mayo native/Who hails from the plain of the yew trees ..." with the strongest implication that he too be allowed to tell the whole truth, having previously explained in Mayo Irish: "If you traverse the talk on the *tóchar Phádraic*/Avoid the *fóidín mearaí*/Attend to the codes once hewn from a tree trunk of yew/And be careful of the truth for fear of the oppressor/I know the Mayo way ..." Again, the references to topographical features, place names and to folkloric beliefs reinforce the intimate connection between landscape, language, culture and identity, wherein place names and cultural readings of landscape may, as Basso points out, "be used to summon forth an enormous range of mental and emotional associations – associations of time and space, of history and events, of persons and social activities, of oneself and stages in one's life". In this Irish context, as the poem shows, such associations are most immediately accessible through indigenous, Irish-language names and terms. In conclusion, the poet co-inhabits Mayo's freedom-fighters, saying triumphantly: "They live forever like the yew tree when we attend to the truth/When we value it, voice it, tell it, and flaunt it like the red and green" (the Mayo colours).

The second poem in the sequence, "A Vote for Love", refers to the marriage equality vote, which has been incorporated into the Irish constitution. Michael says "I grew up gay in Castlebar/Beyond the limits of language/Displaced in the world without words ..." his alienation being due to a lack of speech. (In the poem "Hail and Farewell", the poet shows how the inability to speak – "I can never give that knowledge/voice" – allows the truth to seep out in emotions more appropriate to other circumstances: "There is grief buried deep within/Misplaced ... When I read out loud emotional poems/Sorrow surfaces suddenly in the absent space/Between the words"). The theme of language as a grounding principle, which surfaces in all the poems, gets full expression here. He says, "French literature delivered me salvation ... Saint Genet and Gide and Albert Camus ..." These are the writers who have influenced him, and he ruefully makes a joke against himself about his lack of sunny optimism "[They]Stole creative fire from the gods/To illuminate my inner Mayo ..." which is a wry expression of the real hurt he suffered growing up gay at a time when homosexuality was illegal. I also enjoyed his witty relocation of the Greek myth of Sisyphus, with its Camusian echoes of the absurd: "Of imagining a solitary Sisyphus absurdly happy/Climbing to the top of a cold Croagh Patrick ..."

As a broadcaster, Michael continually references in his poems the human voice as the ultimate means of salvation. For him, the human voice is the privileged medium of meaning. For the first time, the perspective has shifted onto the written word, which gets primacy here: "Book learning that privileged absence/Reader and writer both invoking death/Yet looking to speech as a present possibility ..." What Michael articulates is a clear reflection of the deconstruction philosophy of Jacques Derrida, again invoking salvation delivered by French literature. (Undecidable difference also surfaces in the concluding irony of the poem "Belfast": "And the eventual exodus of English gentry/Leaving us the poorer for their absence/And presence"). Michael says: "Pioneering writers wrote upon my soul/They inscribed the vellum of my skin with sexual traces/They founded me in a reality that fit/They endowed me with a language of affirmation ..." And thus inscribed with Derrida's trace, he presents himself to us as poet by saying, "These words I wear have set me free ..." Of his origins favouring writing, Michael says "My mother wrote yes to love ... She nourished me by writing yes for my lifetime ..." and, "My father wrote yes to me/ He underpinned my being with a covenant ..." "A Vote for Love" captures and reflects the extraordinary openheartedness seen during the campaign for marriage equality in Ireland, in which people of all ages and backgrounds came forward to voice deeply personal stories, experiences and hopes for themselves, their family members and their friends to be recognised as equal, and for that equality to be enshrined in the written text of the Irish Constitution: "The Mammies and the Daddies/the Grandas and the Nanas/Wrote yes: my child is cherished/The same as any other". The poem concludes "The people of Ireland have voted yes for everyone/They accepted into words what was not spoken ... Overturning years of hurtful judgements/In the stroke of a pen ..." And there is relief in this conclusion, which also contains in the word "performance" a nodding reference to the tautological position of religion, which proscribes homosexual acts, even though being requires doing i.e. one cannot call oneself a poet without writing poems: "At long last recognition and performance/For the limitless language of love ..." embracing gender equality. As he notices critically "Only silent churchmen barricaded dusty doors/Against the greening breath of the Holy Spirit/And the swelling surge of sexual truth ..." (In the poem "Complicity", Michael angrily returns to this theme of discrimination: "How do you condemn people who are gay/But hold them in respect and with dignity/When I hear such distinctions/Bullying subtly with buts ... dare I name their rationalisation/An opinion that was formed in advance/Prejudice".)

Finally, in the third poem of the Mayo sequence, which lends its title to this volume, Michael comes to terms with the very recent death of his mother. This poem is hugely emotional, and uses the iconography of Mayo to describe his feelings during the funeral, from the moment of his mother's death to her burial. He has situated this poem at Old Head in Mayo, "Beneath the shadow of Croagh Patrick ..." The poet describes his mother's death in the contrasting terms of a soft, feminine sea, and hard, masculine land. The actual moment of her death is like a nuclear explosion, which changes the landscape: "Weighed down with giving/I watched until you sank/The blast hit before the absent surface calmed/And then I turned and faced the land ..." The poet has to face the future without his mother's presence, and in three brief but profound lines he enumerates what this means: "Stripped of a welcome/No resting place left/With nobody to tell ..." He further draws on the folk-memory of the cruel clearances around Castlebar during the famine, to express his horror and terror at her death: "The crowbar brigade has brought death to a sound foundation/A momentary fearful glimpse of what this clearance means ..." His home is gone, and the foundation of his very being has been reduced to rubble. Succinctly, and very simply, he expresses the profound truth of such an irreplaceable loss: "I have lost someone/who loved me/Unconditionally ..." He mourns the finality of her absence bitterly: "The tide on the turn shovelled up the sand/And you were gone from me/For ever ..." (There are three lines in the poem "Devotion" which reverberate, and reflect light on the magnitude of the grief which Michael feels in relation to the loss of his mother. He says "When I hold you to me in my arms/I carry what is most valuable in all the world/Access to your presence ..." And in the poem "Hail and Farewell", he writes of what is unspeakable: "I kissed her goodbye/And left/I never saw her alive again/I can never give that knowledge/voice".)

Once again the poet describes in religious terms the transfiguring power of love, this time during the daily grind of mothering: "Your effigy infused an ordinary morning/With all the rainbow colours of a mother's love/In an extraordinary daily miracle ..." After viewing his mother's body, Michael says, "I knew you were ordained a saint ..." And he concludes the poem by referring to the apparition at Knock in Mayo in the context of mythological appearances of the goddess "You came to me across the foam ..." In a wonderful loving image of the mother and child, using gesture as speech, he delineates: "You didn't speak but held me in your gaze/As once you cradled your first-born in the curve of an arm ..." The last lines of this poem are not despairing, but draw together the strands of gratitude that permeate it. In the language of flowers, a chaplet of roses signifies beauty and virtue rewarded: "At my feet/A chaplet of roses/Floating gently on the ebb ..." And Michael makes a simple prayer to his mother in heaven: "Thank you/For your legacy/Of love". The two poems about animals in this collection permit the poet a latitude in language. Michael uses the conceit to speak about women, and the misogynistic way they can be represented and spoken about. While telling the story of Tyke the elephant, who was shot by Hawaiian police after making a break for freedom, he writes: "The female died in a hail of gunfire/Because she would not accept/Being imprisoned in a circus/Wearing ridiculous costumes/Turning tricks for man's amusement/For twenty years she suffered the insistent cruelty of clowns ..." The ironic implication in the title of the poem, "Bad Behaviour Can Get Elephants Killed", is that the female must remain under male control: "The public must be protected/From a female on the rampage ... Because of her intelligence/And her memory/And the bigness of her heart". And he delivers the closing lines with the masculine certainty of a public news conference: "She had to be put down/No question": the matter is closed; now, let's move on. In another poem which draws sustenance from the Billy Wilder film *Some Like It Hot*, Michael writes about a chocolate Labrador called Toga. Because he is referring to a dog, he is able to say things about the battle of the sexes in comedic language redolent of the Prohibition era: "And what do you make of her behaviour/Coming in at two o'clock in the morning/Some tramp from God knows where/ 'Honey, I forgot the time ...' Slut/Charging down the hall/And launching herself from the top step/Onto Terry in the bed/Licking him all over/Slurp slurp slurp like her last drink in some cheap speakeasy/You think a kiss will make this better?" The word "slut", meaning a slovenly or sexually promiscuous woman, is over six hundred years old. Though not used in polite, politically correct speech today, it is clear that Michael knows that the word "slut" also refers to a female dog, pointing to the historical denigration of women through their categorisation in derogatory, animalistic terms as a practice which endures in the present, even if the terminology has changed.

While writing an "Email to ISIS", Michael courageously posits the foreclosure of women, particularly by all religions, as the root cause of evil and insanity: "You blank them with burqas/Negating their existence ... They must have a male chaperone/Otherwise you throw them off the highest building", demonstrating the true value they are accorded. He then asks a rhetorical question "How could you be sane/With your suppression of women/Your refusal of the feminine side of your nature".

Through the labyrinth of language, Michael Murphy is sure-footed, although he recognises that language is problematic. The love poem "Devotion" manifests the instability of language. In the phrase, "So thank you for choosing me/To love/To be intimate with", the apparent one-sided gratitude expressed for being chosen, which can be an unacceptable burden, is exploded in the next line, "to love". The verb refers to both the lover, but also to the person loved, who has been released through that choosing to love in return. Michael writes about the subject of language in the poem "The Seeker". As a poet, he says he is "... a seeker after truth/Shooting arrows at a moving target/Capturing truth with an onslaught of words/Whose whittled tips sink home/With the exploding poison of emotional recognition ..." In the word "poison" the poet is recognising that the truth can be deadly, and also be open to dispute: curing or killing. As he says, his endeavour is "To create a language barrier/Both protective and offensive/A problematic personal reality/Open to challenge and dispute/Because you do not see me/From the place where I see you ..." Informed by his work as a psychoanalyst, Michael is speaking about the truth of subjectivity which is not a universal truth, but a particular one unique to each individual. He recognises that the truth is not a given fully formed, but is constructed in the dialectical movement between two people, meaningful only in the context of language: "I need you to help me/Tell the truth/Lacking your support/I lie/I speak false ..." His conclusion is prayer, a pleading:

"... let us be true to one another/Striking the target/Together".

In another poem, "Repetition", he refers to free-floating anxiety arising from "A linguistic net of language/That catches insignificant gnats ... Ties me up in knots" with the pun on "nots", indicating that his negation – the "inner Mayo" that he spoke about elsewhere – is due to fear. There is a phrase full of insight counteracting that anxiety in this poem, which bears fruitful meditation. Referring to the past, the poet realises "Yet everything that has happened/Is the same: it just happened on different days ..."

In the poem "Seven", Michael captures the full meaning of the inability to speak, the absence of speech, through the story of Dermot, who witnessed the death of his friend when they both were seven years of age. It was a traumatic incident which left Dermot with a bad stammer. With empathic understanding the poet writes, "Later on when bullies mocked me/Co-copied my st-stammer/I stood there frozen unable to say/Anything back quick-fire/Some devastating put-down/That began without a vowel/Or a consonant just a hard scream/So I thumped my attackers ..." Even though the poet is speaking about children, he is showing that the inability to speak leads to an acting out through physical violence. The words "frozen" and "thump" are a repeat. They recall the poet's earlier use of the words: "My friend frozen in the road/I heard the thump the screaming brakes/The pumping blood red/When I was seven ..." which links the acting out to that devastating trauma. Throughout, Michael is using language that a child would us, frozen at that seven years of age.

Michael's joy in the use of language extends even into the local vernacular: "As I swaddle you with wealthy words from Cork ..." A glorious poem called "My Perfect Ruby" references a newborn through the alchemist's term for the elixir of life. It was written for his Cork friends on the occasion of the birth of their child, named Ruby, and he employs slang words from Cork to increase the sense of intimacy at this happy time, and uses the rhythmic lilt and phrasing of the Cork accent. "C'mere my perfect Ruby/You took us by surprise girl/When you landed here la/Da berries – a welcome gift like – on-real/ Look at the gatch of you/Lying on your back with your doonchie arms in the air/A bold Cork ball-hopper all balmed out ..." "Da berries" means the best happening; "the gatch" refers to the gait or personal deportment; "doonchie" means tiny; a "ball-hopper" refers to a mischievously humorous person; and "balmed out" is lying down, especially while sun-bathing, even in a mother's love.

In the poem "Bread", the poet uses conversational language to express the implied loneliness behind the breaking of bread at a meal: "Bread is such a shared pleasure/The sheer goodness of it/ Don't waste it/Eat up while you can/There are people starving/ Did I thank you for inviting me". Expatriates can feel isolated in the poet's beloved Spain, the location of this poem about sharing bread: "Have you had it with salt and olive oil ..." In the poem "Figs and Blue Cheese", the poet contrasts the urban, impermanent holiday-land of sun umbrellas, with the rural, down-to-earth Spanish way they have always done things, through referring to "Figs and blue cheese/Waiting on Wedgwood plates/Under a white sun umbrella ..." and "Salty cheese and succulent figs/Overflow a cracked Cartuja plate/Under an ancient olive tree ..." He ends the poem on a surprising note: "A gift today for you and me/To share with love and be inspired by". His use of the shimmering phrase "and be inspired by" is perfect in context, because for over seven hundred years "gift" has had the specialised meaning in English of "inspiration", which survives today in the word "gifted", meaning naturally talented. In the poem "Email to ISIS", Michael asks "Or will those few left alive .../Be refugees fleeing the handiwork of a barbarian". The original meaning of "barbarian" referred to non-Christians, especially Muslims, which was gradually replaced by the meaning uncultured and ignorant, so that the poet's use of this particular word also references the underlying theme of the poem: "I see you have a passion for ignorance".

There is also a theme of valediction in many of the poems of this collection. In the tender poem "Enough", the poet writes, "Of that sundering moment of change/When I shall fall through your loosening fingers/Like water/An exhalation towards the ultimate/Setting me and our love story free forever/To soar over an ocean of grief ..." Michael expresses the brutal practicality of dealing with death in the poem "I Shall Die": "The pictures I collected the china I chose/The book I was reading my toothbrush/Stuff to be binned with the dead body in the bed". And he tackles the same subject of death in a humorous fashion in the poem "Interruption". Here he is writing once again on the subject of language: "I think I should sit down for death/Such an ill-mannered interruption/Deserves to be received seated/To place a full stop in mid-sentence/Is offensive and meaningless ..." And the conclusion is delightfully ambiguous, where rudeness is happily entered into: "Nevertheless I shall sit down for Death/As a personal protest/To uphold a standard of behaviour/Since I do know better/Good manners should matter/At least to me ..." (Humour is also a theme running through these poems, notably in the poem "Kiwi": "The kiwi is such an unnecessary fruit/About as useful as a decorative kumquat"). In the poem "Relationships Do Not Die", Michael uses a round to emphasize the continuation of life after death, in a further version of that imaginative "co-(in)-habitation" about which I spoke earlier. The poem begins "Relationships do not die with death/They live on in our bones". It concludes with the statement "They die only when I die". This apparent finality is immediately altered by a repetition of the glossing refrain "Relationships do not die with death/they live on in our bones", meaning that those who survive him will carry forward the relationship in an unending cycle.

The poet boldly advocates rudeness as self-affirmation in the poem "On Turning Sixty-five", with his "... everything to do list ...", which may take people aback, but there is hard-earned and healthy psychological wisdom in what this poet advocates: "Revolt and don't comply/Become an annoying individual/Drop people who aren't supportive/Love the few/Be truthfully rude to interfering relatives …" This is the advice with which viewers of his psychoanalytic-residency on the RTÉ afternoon television show will be familiar, and which holds out the promise of relief from carrying unnecessary burdens thrust upon us by the strictures of politeness or duty.

A Chaplet of Roses is a continuation of a journey begun in The Republic of Love, which navigates the territories of deep feeling and experience through the vehicle of language. If, as Michael has pointed out, language is a net in which it is possible to become tangled, the poems here demonstrate that it is also a web that weaves threads of connection between individuals and communities, expressing and underlining the interconnectedness of past, present and future, most especially through the enduring nature of love in its many manifestations. In its observations and explorations of themes which touch on many facets of human experience, Michael's poetry expresses truths at once deeply personal and universal in their resonances; it opens for the reader and listener a sense of place, at once unique and shared, which it invites us to occupy and cohabit along with our fellow travellers. His poems continue to flower in the heart and mind long after we close the pages of this beautiful book. In return, I quote the prayer of the poet's concluding words: "Thank you/For your legacy/Of love".

Dr Jeannine Woods
School of Languages, Literatures and Cultures,
National University of Ireland, Galway, 2015

Flora and Fauna …

And When You Speak of Trees

I plant a tiny tree in crumbling earth
And make an investment
In someone else's future

When I leave this world
I know my representative will be a mighty oak
With wide-spreading penetrating roots
And branches that can soar into the sky's embrace
A worthwhile legacy to have left behind me

It signifies that I believe in a life hereafter
That I believe in you whom I've never met
A leap of faith that you shall care for trees
And the animals and birds who live within its leafy shelter

In an unimaginable future
You too shall be my representative on earth
You shall speak up for trees
Even though you never knew
That I was the one who dug the hole
Loosened the roots and gently settled the ball down into clay
And staked the sapling's stem
When it was my time under the sun

You shall be my voice as well
To husband what I had intended

Your time is now when living is all
And love I hope that you found love
In your relationship with trees
As I did once in mine
It turns out that love is the firmest groundwork of our being
With roots to anchor truth
That love grows up to be a mighty oak tree
Linking the earth to the heavens
And those who have gone before to the present generation
With no beginning and no projected end
An oak tree is eternity for an everyday

And when you speak of trees and give them breath
A breeze will move imperceptibly through clacking branches
Listen then to the chattering whisper of their leaves
You'll find that trees have the ability to soothe the soul
With their conversation
With their assured presence
With their sudden silences
With their waiting
For humble trees are wise
They tap deep into the earth
They remind us when we're inundated by life's political trivia
Of the one enduring strength that truly matters
The unconditional love that surrounds us
Love that can be seen and heard in oak trees
In those who planted them
And in those others who will tend
To help them grow to independence

Anna's Dog Toga

I believe a dog should be a he
A suitable companion for a man
Terry corrects me "Toga is a she!"
So I told him I prefer to think of her
As trans-gendered like Bruce Jenner

Mind you from behind
She walks like a model
Toe first heel next
Waggling her booty like jello
From side to side

Though from the front
Her hind legs are as powerful
As a rugby player's in a ruck
Try taking her out for a sedate stroll
On the scent for overlooked pieces of bread

And what do you make of her behaviour
Coming in at two o'clock in the morning
Some tramp from God knows where
"Honey, I forgot the time ..." Slut
Charging down the hall
And launching herself from the top step
Onto Terry in the bed licking him all over
Slurp slurp slurp like her last drink in some cheap speakeasy
You think a kiss will make this better?
As beautiful as Marilyn in the striptease spotlight
Who could refuse her anything?

Nevertheless I keep getting the fuzzy end of the lollipop
I think I'll sue for loss of consortium

She has to be gay
Or at the very least bisexual
Maybe she's a lesbian
A he or a she or a tranny
As Osgood said "Well, nobody's perfect!"

A chocolate Labrador named Toga
Whose soulful looks melt all before her
Whose motivation is food and hunting cats
And two paw hugs retrieving hearts
Loved and shared by Anna and by Terry
And luckily by me for being the shadow's chosen one
Two females who are loved by two males
A perfect foursome family

Bad Behaviour Can Get Elephants Killed

Animals do not belong to us
They allow us to live near them
And bad behaviour can get elephants killed

I saw Tyke an African elephant
Running free in 1994
Through the business streets of Honolulu
Not on the tropical savannahs of home
Before Hawaiian police shot her dead
With eighty-seven bullets
In front of horrified bystanders
One went in through the eye
Never to be forgotten

The elephant and us
We saw too much
Of man's inhumanity
To fellow creatures

The female died in a hail of gunfire
Because she would not accept
Being imprisoned in a circus
Wearing ridiculous costumes
Turning tricks for man's amusement

For twenty years she suffered the insistent cruelty of clowns
Then she lashed out and killed a trainer
She had to be put down
No question

The public must be protected
From a female on the rampage
Especially an elephant
Because of her intelligence
And her memory
And the bigness of her heart

Animals do not belong to us
They allow us to live near them
To be graced by their honour
To learn from their integrity
To encourage gentleness
And lay hold of tenderness
To allow ourselves to love them
And be loved a hundredfold in return
Only then can we appreciate and fight for freedom
For everyone

Animals do not belong to us
They allow us to live near them
And bad behaviour can get elephants killed

Poems for Friends ...

This poem was written for my friends, Dermot Byrne and Fiona O'Boyle, on the occasion of their wedding, Holy Thursday, 17 April 2014. Dermot hails from Knockbridge in County Louth, and Fiona is from Clacton-on-Sea, of Irish parentage.

Seven

When I was seven
I deliberately kicked the ball into the road
When I was seven

And my friend ran after it
When I was seven

Too late I saw the roaring truck
My friend frozen in the road
I heard the thump the screaming brakes
The pumping blood red
When I was seven

And I saw that it was all my fault
When I was seven

They could not put him together again – no
My best friend – no
When I was seven

They said that he was now an angel
Because I kicked the ball out into the road
When I was seven

He was me and I was he
My best friend who ran away
And went to heaven without me
When I was seven

And I thought that I could never speak again
Ever again
never again
I lost my voice
When I was seven

Later on when bullies mocked me
Co-copied my st-stammer
I stood there frozen unable to say
Anything back quick-fire
Some devastating put-down
That began without a vowel
Or a consonant just a hard scream
So I thumped my attackers
But each time I died a little more
Inside

And then when I was forty-seven
I recognised my best friend
When I was forty-seven

She was kind and good with children
She took all the time to hear me
And I began to speak again
When I was forty-seven

I knew that I would never have to stammer in her presence
Ever again
Forever
When I was forty-seven

I am able to say
My voice came back
When I was forty-seven

So I said yes to you
Yes I do
Yes I will
It took only a breath yes
And it was easy
For love never dies between a boy and his best friend

This Easter the two of us are risen from the dead
A man has regained his voice through an angel from heaven
Dressed in white and holding a bouquet of seven red roses

We have promised to protect each other with love
On our journey towards the future
For seven times seven years
Or for as long as the time will allow

So side by side talking together
Me and my best friend
We walk deliberately now
Out into the open road

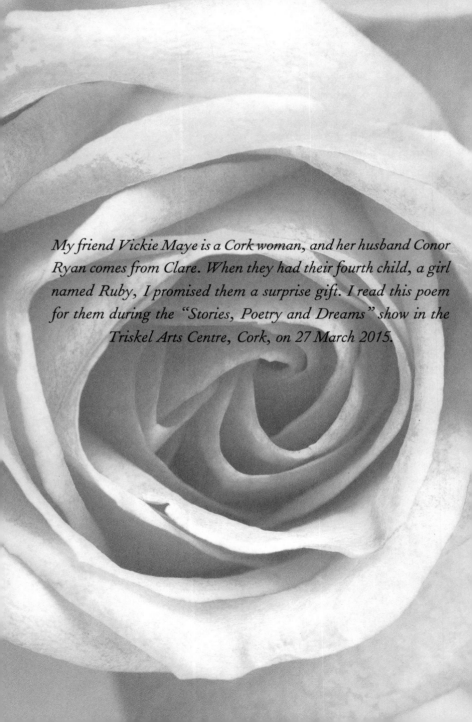

My friend Vickie Maye is a Cork woman, and her husband Conor Ryan comes from Clare. When they had their fourth child, a girl named Ruby, I promised them a surprise gift. I read this poem for them during the "Stories, Poetry and Dreams" show in the Triskel Arts Centre, Cork, on 27 March 2015.

My Perfect Ruby

When I looked you in the eye
My perfect Ruby
I knew that you were here
To cure diseases
To change base metal into bars of gold
And to prolong my life indefinitely
A panacea
She lamped at me and said
"See ya
On Pana!"

More precious than diamonds
I cupped your head in my hand
As you thrust into the cradle of my love
Glowing red hot with life
Supping at my breast
And I named you Ruby Ryan
After your dad
Who did the same

C'mere my perfect Ruby –
You took us by surprise girl
When you landed here la –
Da berries – a welcome gift like – on-real

Look at the gatch of you
Lying on your back with your doonchie arms in the air
A bold Cork ball-hopper all balmed out

And from the tocht in my throat
I knew my perfect Ruby
I just knew that as a family
When your ship arrived into the safe harbour of our Lee-side shore
That we were all haunted like

As I swaddle you with wealthy words from Cork
My desire for you girl
Is to create a limitless world of possibilities
In which you can play happily for an eternity
To construct a safe reality ring o' rosie round you
Chainied up with loving language
From your mam and from your dad
That you can trust implicitly

Where as much as we can make it happen
You will be free to be yourself forever
To love and break boys' hearts on Barracka
And to be loved unconditionally in return

My wish is as a young ruby woman
Blazing with light and rich with the Cork colours
You'll never have to comply nor compromise yourself
Or worse withdraw from all that life's adventure has to offer
My hope is when you fly the nest
You'll inhabit your heritage
And soar with widespread wings of unconcern
To become a true rebel always
My perfect Ruby
O precious daughter of mine

She lamped at me again and laughed
"C'mon boy willa chalk it down!
Amn't I the bulb off you both?
And amn't I ever —
Up the rebels! —
A proud daughter
Of Cork"

On Food ...

Bread

For Jayne in Spain

Bread should be a shared pleasure
Preferably with a loved one
Breaking a loaf open
You have to taste some of this
Delicious
Smell it
What do you think

Thank you for being here with me
For making the loneliness go away for a moment
For letting me laugh and cry
Try that black one there
Is it rye with molasses maybe?
Have you had it with salt and olive oil?
Isn't bread such a shared pleasure

I can hardly ask these questions of myself
At home on my own
I never buy bread to eat all alone
Staring at the wall in my kitchen
Listening for the cat
Waiting for the mobile phone to ring
I do sometimes wait I mean
For an invitation to go visit
Bread is such a shared pleasure
The sheer goodness of it
Don't waste it

Eat up while you can
There are people starving
Did I thank you for inviting me?

Oh they've brought us a new basket
Hot crusty bread wrapped up in a napkin
You really must have some of this
Go on even a little piece
I love to see the crumbs
The way it breaks apart
I'd eat bread every day if I was able
At someone else's table if I could
Wouldn't that be heavenly
Sat here with a friend
Who cares like you
Bread is such a shared pleasure

Figs and Blue Cheese

Figs and blue cheese
Waiting on Wedgwood plates
Under a white sun umbrella
A table set by the pool
Swimming in summer heat

Salty cheese and succulent figs
Overflow a cracked Cartuja plate
Under an ancient olive tree
Shading a rough board from the scalding sun
Capturing each delicate breeze as ever

Ripe green figs and strong blue cheese
Tasting sweet and crunchy creamy
An eternal offering from the gods
A gift today for you and me
To share with love and be inspired by

The Kiwi

I think the kiwi
Such an unnecessary fruit
Like an unripe green tomato
The last piece of a salad
To be left behind in a bowl
An unlovely rejected afterthought
To be scraped into the bin

I grew up without the kiwi
So why should I include it now
In my food
In my environment

Kiwis arrived in England in the fifties
But I never remember them in Castlebar
A sliced addition to a tired leaf of lettuce
Winking repulsively like a gleaming eye
Desiring to be eaten alive

The kiwi is such an unnecessary fruit
About as useful as a decorative kumquat

On Death and Dying ...

I Shall Die

There will come a time
When I shall die
And be obliterated

On that momentous day
Which will matter to no one else but me
The meaning I gave to the furniture of my life
Will fade with my ghost

The pictures I collected the china I chose
The book I was reading my toothbrush
Stuff to be binned with the dead body in the bed

I was an unimportant person
The generation who met me
Freed from duty
Will soon forget

Nevertheless I was loved once
By someone special
And I loved him in return
We glimpsed eternity together
Before all traces of existence
Were wiped away by oblivion

Thirty years ago, John was a client of my partner Terry. When he was diagnosed with inoperable brain cancer, he returned to Ireland from America, and he sought Terry's help once more, eventually becoming a friend. John loved "The Poppy" poem, and read it every night for as long as he was able, and he had pride of place at the launch of The Republic of Love. *When he was very ill, in those dying days, John asked Terry if I would write a poem especially for him, to serve as a remembrance. I had the privilege of reading "Enough" to John in the company of his wife, Mia.*

Enough

These are the final days
Trembling on the brink
Before my life
And what we have done together
The love story we have made
Overflows into eternity

I feel sadness
At having to leave that love behind
Love was all that mattered
In the end

And I regret my abandonment
Of you and me
Facing into this final act
That I shall do unusually alone

Death will happen to me unbeknownst
For once without my love
Fiercely protecting me to that uttermost breath
Beyond exhaustion
And the sudden unexpected silence
Of that sundering moment of change
When I shall flow through your loosening fingers
Like water
An exhalation towards the ultimate
Setting me and our love story free forever
To soar over an ocean of grief

I shall surprise you at times
And overwhelm you at others
But it's me just saying "Hi there!"
As our loving memories re-play on a loop
Without ever ceasing

I shall breathe you in my love
With my last living breath
And take the strength of your glorious spirit with me
Into eternity

But I shall need to say when I'm gone
What you cannot bear to hear
That the two of us
You and me
That we have done
Enough

Interruption

I think I should sit down for death
Such an ill-mannered interruption
Deserves to be received seated

To place a full stop in mid-sentence
Is offensive and meaningless
It leaves me nonplussed

Patching tentative presence onto such an absence
Voicing into the void
Attempting to cover over the hole in existence
With a tissue of words and phrases
Sounds courageous
Even foolhardy
But bound to rend
Inevitably
Finally

Nevertheless I shall sit down for Death
As a personal protest
To uphold a standard of behaviour
Since I do know better

Good manners should matter
At least to me

Hail and Farewell

There is grief buried deep within
Misplaced pain heavy and burdensome

When I read out loud emotional poems
Sorrow surfaces suddenly in the absent space
Between the words
Ave atque vale

I have difficulty holding on
Holding back
Riven
Hiccupping inappropriate sobs
A fury of stinging tears
Heartbroken
I never knew I was

When I listen to music
Bach beautifully rendered
Returned restored handed over
I cry at so munificent a gift
When I hear a brass band
I laugh and weep together
At the trumpeting valour
Head held high pennants flying
Terry doesn't mind anymore
I don't know why that happens

When I packed the car in Spain
For the journey home
Toga the Labrador my shadow
Was absent
I found her sunk in the well of the car
At the passenger seat where I usually sat
Woebegone
She knew what parting meant
She sensed my heart breaking
Broken
Take me with you
I embraced her
And she licked my beard

When my mother died
She was ninety-five
Sleeping and not eating
A tiny figure curled among the pillows
With her head resting into her shoulder
Like a famished fledgling *scalltán*
I kissed her goodbye
And left
I never saw her alive again
I can never give that knowledge
Voice

Relationships Do Not Die

Relationships do not die with death
They live on in our bones
They are a part of who we are each day
Participating in the conversation
Living still
Whispering

Their shades visit while we are asleep
In search of home
Renewing feelings from the past
Enabling us to face the future
In the present
Helping with their gifts

I can forgive and accept them for who they were
I do not feel diminished by who they thought I was
They are alive
Always benevolent
They die only when I die

Relationships do not die with death
They live on in our bones

Some Personal Poems ...

The Seeker

I am a seeker after truth
Shooting arrows at a moving target
Capturing truth with an onslaught of words
Whose whittled tips sink home
With the exploding poison of emotional recognition

Refining my aim over time
I have improved in my endeavour
To build a layering of phrases
To create a language barrier
Both protective and offensive
A problematic personal reality
Open to challenge and dispute
Because you do not see me
From the place where I see you

Situate in that resistant gulf
Exposed to instant judgement
No regard for wisdom earned
Irrelevant as a used hankie
I can lose my certain footing
And fall forever in infinite space
Without another's holding lifeline

Truth requires the two of us
Communicating in a hail
Of shooting arrows building up
Or taking down word by word
I need you to help me

Tell the truth
Lacking your support
I lie
I speak false

Overcome my reticence
Shoot arrows at my heart
Seek me out my love
As I have sought out you
And let us be true to one another
Striking arrows at the target
Together

On Turning Sixty-five

Nothing to prove
Nothing to lose
An everything to do list:

Insist on being here
Write
Creatively play every day
Stay offline
Embrace an electronic sunset

Don't follow time
Potter
Have a project
Life-long learning top of the agenda
Art and literature
Listening to classical music

Revolt and don't comply
Become an annoying individual
Drop people who aren't supportive
Love the few
Be truthfully rude to interfering relatives
And take the time to contemplate
Life and death without regret or bitterness
Enjoy the holiday here
Always
Or at least
For as long as possible
And live today eternally

Bereft

I feel bereft of God
No resting place left for my idealism
No deity to invoke
No divine being to call upon for help

When Helen and her sister attended a Catholic Mass
The standing and the sitting the incense and solemnity
They got the giggles: "Presbyterians sit and pray!" they complained
I'd never seen the spectacle as ridiculous before
Which it is – and a waste of time – if you don't believe

At least I have the language still
To express impossible truths and capture the ineffable
To underpin my life with meaningful myths
The birth of immanence
The crucifixion of truth
The resurrection of hope
And perhaps that final stage of growing up
The ascension to mature human responsibility
Without the joyful presence of my God
With all the sharp-eyed clarity of a Presbyterian elder

Belfast

Yesterday I went up to Belfast
There were churches on practically every street
With unfamiliar names like Moravian and Plymouth Brethren

In Sainsbury's supermarket in Sprucefield
They had short-crust pastry pies
Foods that we would never even think of eating

A lot of the white people's facial types were very different
Alien to my eyes foreign

Belfast must be populated with the relics of empire
What Dublin was like once
In the time of James Joyce
Before we became an independent people's republic
And the eventual exodus of English gentry
Leaving us the poorer for their absence
And presence

Complicity

Were I to remain silent
Where there is injustice
I would be complicit in a crime

How can you consider that black and white are equal
But treat them as separate nonetheless
How can you regard women the same as men
But still insist that they have different roles to play
How do you condemn people who are gay
But hold them in respect and with dignity

When I hear such distinctions
Bullying subtly with buts
Do I not recognise
The suffering of one like me
Do I not reach out
To shield from shame
My brother my sister myself
And dare I name their rationalisation
An opinion that was formed in advance
Prejudice

Email to ISIS

Hi ISIS

I see you have a passion for ignorance
Which is why you behead people
To cleanse the world of knowledge

Because you consider culture a decadent concept
You blow up works of art
To obliterate antiquities and the past

Since for you women are less than men
You blank them with burqas
Negating their existence
Confining them behind closed doors

If women bring children to school
They must have a male chaperone
Otherwise you throw them off the highest building
In the name of Allah the most merciful
A god who according to you demands human sacrifice
And the rape and murder of apostates and infidels

You know, ISIS, it's the usual story of religion
From the history you excised
The Crusaders, the Catholic Monarchs,
Cromwell, the Inquisition
The intolerant have always engaged in wars of religion
I wish we had grown up a little more

And abandoned those primitive opinions
For that is what they are: paradoxical ideas
That are true and not true at the same time
Undecidable metaphors that some people choose to live by
Which helps them to be healthy human beings

I regret to say you're nothing special
People like you have always existed
Hitler and Stalin Pol Pot and Mao Tse Tung
Kim Jong Il and Isaias Afwerki in Eritrea
Tyrants who take their peoples hostage
And experiment with terror and mass murder

When you have finished
Re-making the world in your image yet again
Turning this verdant earth into a barren desert
May I ask will there be room in your creation
For those who sing and dance
And sculpt and paint and make music
Write with beautiful words and tell emotional stories
Who value the human spirit
The freedom of the imagination
Who take delight in the plurality of peoples
Who place their trust in love and live their dream
Or will those few left alive who vehemently disagree with you
Be refugees fleeing the handiwork of a barbarian

I feel sorry for your parents
Who found a welcome refuge in Europe
You have rejected the opportunities they gave you
Returning to the poverty they fled
How can they be proud of what you have now become
A dangerous deluded madman

Psychotically certain of your righteousness
In need of serious intervention

I can see why you wield such control
You are terrified of what's inside you
Of what's inside each one of us
You torture others with the blackness in your own soul
Externalise the evil at your core
In a desperate attempt to save yourself
Blaming God for giving in to badness
Needless to say I don't believe in your justification

How could you be sane
With your suppression of women
Your refusal of the feminine side of your nature

The greatest contribution I can make to humanity
Is to manage myself in a positive way
Allowing others do the same in their way
At their own pace accepting difference
I dare not let your madness contaminate me
I need strong boundaries to protect myself
For lunacy is alive like quicksand
If I walk in there I'll drown

Health is a personal journey undertaken within
An ethical achievement to be worked for day by day
Hardly made easy by going overseas to Syria
It's not a simple task but a worthwhile endeavour
The benefits are felt daily in my dealings with people

So I appeal to the best in you
Even though I know you cannot hear me

Imprisoned as you are in your passion for ignorance
I hope you that will find peace
Eventually

Michael

Repetition

When there's no alternative
I'll try again

I have made wrong decisions in my life
And I am scalded with regrets
About the past

About what has not happened in the future
Continuing on till infirmity or death
I feel fear

Yet everything that has happened
Is the same: it just happened on different days

Free floating anxiety
Not tied down to something specific
Ties me up in knots
A linguistic net of language
That catches insignificant gnats
Over and over again

I survived and got myself to here
By finding solutions to actual problems
Practically as they happened to me

Why do I forget that truth
Continually

Devotion

I am devoted to you
This motivation gives meaning to my life
It has illumined everything I do

So thank you for choosing me
To love
To be intimate with
To carry like a cloak
The reflection of your open soul

Where there is love
Despair does not venture in
Where there is affection
Forgiveness happens unbeknownst
Where there is laughter
We are equal and as one

When I caress your face with my finger
Trace the delicate hairs of your eyelids
Touch your lips with the gentlest kiss
Embrace your strong body
When I hold you to me in my arms
I carry what is most valuable in all the world
Access to your presence

I benefit from that burden
It clears a pathway for me through life's dangers
To your heart

I shine in the light of your acute mind
I see myself reflected in your gaze
I hear myself at home in your kindly speech

Inspired by those blessings
I can occupy my chosen place
Caring for your well-being

To become a unique individual
Different from you
Connected loosely
Yet solidly belonging

The two of us transfigured
By the deepening of intimacy
And the abundant flowering of our love

The Mayo Sequence ...

The Irish for Mayo is Maigh Eo, meaning "the plain of the yew trees". The motto on the County Mayo coat of arms is "Dia is Muire linn", God and Mary be with us. A meitheal is a group of neighbours and friends who come together to help each other out for a day or two. Tóchar Phádraic means Patrick's Causeway, an ancient pilgrimage route that runs from Ballintubber Abbey to Ireland's holy mountain, Croagh Patrick. A fóidín mearaí, literally "a sod of confusion", is a piece of unstable turf that could lead you astray.

Home to Mayo

I am a Mayo man born and bred
I have the character of a Mayo native
Who hails from the plain of the yew trees

My ancient roots are silently asleep
Beneath the brown blanket bog of Ballycroy
Untold ages of my Mayo ancestors
Are compressed within my tight-grained rings
Their umbilical-corded branches linking clay with sky
Have combined in a stout *meitheal*
To grow a dark indomitable tree that is eternally evergreen
Whose flattened leaves reach heavenwards in the racing Mayo light
Protecting those who went before
On their climbing pilgrimage home

I am a dowsing rod of yew
I am the resurrection welling up
From successive imprints on my soul
They have written their names on my body
Like the ancient ogham inscriptions on the standing stones
Of Erris and Murrisk and Costello
A shin bone with five fingers across it meaning "I: the yew tree"
We have survived through countless lifetimes
In the nine baronies of Mayo

Green sapwood for the tension
Red heartwood for compression
Wood that is gnarled and tough

And as mightily resilient as the people of Mayo have had to be
These are my people
This is my place
We have renewed like the yew tree over thousands of years

Mayo handseled me the flame of life
I stand indebted for that gift of highest value
The flesh of your flesh in an eternal relay
Mayo people I know instinctively from deep within
Today it is my turn to give them voice
To make known in my living all of their untold stories
For the West is awake in me
I am a Mayo man born and bred
I have the character of a Mayo native
Who hails from the plain of the yew trees

Though I left the county years ago for work around the world
I could never settle or commit to life elsewhere
Inside I always feel an outsider misplaced
In my mind I always live at home in Mayo

Welcomed home now for the Christmas
By a candle in the window decked with green holly red berries
Or maybe wondering in London or Boston
In Toronto or Melbourne
Is there snow on Neiphin or abroad on the top of Mweelrea

Building summer sandcastles now at Keel in Achill with the next
    generation
Walking the golden beach at Old Head with the previous one
Or maybe crowding into foreign bars
Proudly flying the red and green amongst expatriate Irish
Almost afraid to watch Mayo in the final

Trying their utmost giving of their best yet again
Unwilling to submit to a surrender

Mostly I miss the warm embrace of the Mayo accent
That kiss on the lips blowing in off the Atlantic with the sea spray
Soft and fierce and salty easy
Mayo talk is a baptism that strengthens my spirit
It fills me with hope and immerses me in certainty
It welcomes me into the family of like-minded people
I feel wrapped up in the arms of Croagh Patrick surrounding Clew Bay
With the church at the summit worn aslant
Carried at a typical angle of western defiance

I'm aware that spoken words in Mayo
Mean more than what they say
There are many layered voices speaking
If you traverse the talk on the *tóchar Phádraic*
Avoid the *fóidín mearaí*
Attend to the codes once hewn from a tree trunk of yew
And be careful of the truth for fear of the oppressor
I know the Mayo way
I have climbed the Reek *Dia is Muire linn*

I remember especially those faithful Mayo patriots
Who fought for their freedom at the Races of Castlebar
First citizen President John Moore's republic
Founded on being free to tell the whole truth without fear
And with liberty fraternity equality for all
Their voices were suppressed and silenced by the enemy
Their unwavering Mayo spirit is alive and can never be defeated
Their souls are resurrected when Mayo wins
Their souls are resurrected when Mayo loses
They are alive in us when we give of the best in ourselves

They live forever like the yew tree when we attend to the truth
When we value it, voice it, tell it, and flaunt it like the red and green
For their memory's sake we can never permit a default or defeat
Today in the Mayo capital of Castlebar
We owe them the freedom to speak in the fullness of truth
To let each Mayoman have his say without fear in this republic

I am a Mayo man born and bred
I have the character of a Mayo native
Who hails from the plain of the yew trees
Today I have renewed my yew tree roots
Today I have reclaimed my Mayo heritage
These are my people
This is my place
Today I have come home
To Mayo

The people of Ireland voted yes in the marriage equality referendum of Friday, 22 May 2015, and became the first country in the world to do so by popular vote. Senator Dr Katherine Zappone and her spouse, Dr Ann Louise Gilligan, have been pursuing recognition of their Canadian marriage through the Irish court system since 2004. Their long campaign led to the eventual referendum on same-sex marriage, which was carried by 62 per cent of the electorate.

A Vote for Love

The people of Ireland have voted for me
A homosexual man
They recognised my place
They set me in a broad street

Irish people brought the new law into being
That I have an equal right
To marry the person of my choice
They redeemed the word love in humanity's constitution

The Mammies and the Daddies
The Grandpas and the Nanas
Wrote yes: my child is cherished
The same as any other

My mother wrote yes to love
She affirmed her love for her son
That it was unconditional
She nourished me by writing yes for my lifetime

My father wrote yes to me
He underpinned my being with a covenant
A solemn agreement handed on
From father to son

I grew up gay in Castlebar
Beyond the limits of language

Displaced in a world without words
A disgraced outsider
Shamed by my nameless desires

French literature delivered me salvation
Book learning that privileged absence
Reader and writer both invoking death
Yet looking to speech as a present possibility

Saint Genet and Gide and Albert Camus
Stole creative fire from the gods
To illuminate my inner Mayo
With Mediterranean descriptions
Of illegal sexual encounters underground

Of beautiful male bodies
Swimming provocatively in summer heat
Of exotic Parisian queens
Trailing miracles of the baroque like furbelows
Of imagining a solitary Sisyphus absurdly happy
Climbing to the top of a cold Croagh Patrick

Pioneering writers wrote upon my soul
They inscribed the vellum of my skin with sexual traces
They founded me in a reality that fit
They endowed me with a language of affirmation
They grounded me in fraternity
As one who is equal to another

These words I wear have set me free
They worked on mothers and fathers
Constituency by constituency

On those young people home to vote
Gathered on board their boat
Sailing into Dublin singing
"She moved through the fair …"

They flew from Ghana and Los Angeles
To cast a ballot for their faggot family
From Hong Kong and San Francisco
To demand freedom for their queer friends
I watched the televised map turn green
As the chakra of the heart began to flow

The floodgates of Dublin Castle opened after the vote
And a rainbow of language inundated Dame Street
Men holding hands with men
Women holding hands with women
Men and women holding hands
Lovers out in public walking above ground

They came from north and south and east and west
Linking chains of cheering men and women
Celebrating absence presence difference sameness
Dancing waving kissing embracing crying
A cacophony of car horns and sirens blaring
The unstoppable tide of a proud nation
Urging forward into welcoming acceptance
Joy radiating outwards into the relief of speech
At last a manumission and release of fellow prisoners
At long last recognition and performance
For the limitless language of love
Only silent churchmen barricaded dusty doors
Against the greening breath of the Holy Spirit
And the swelling surge of sexual truth

It was a Katherine and Ann Louise day
Who asked to have their Canadian marriage
Recognised by Irish courts a decade ago
A love they both proclaimed and named
A life they proudly lived out loud
They asked just to be included
Not to be erased by a knowing consensus
On that joyous Saturday all the people approved
The two women threw their open hearts to the audience
And we caught them gratefully
Overturning years of hurtful judgements
In the stroke of a pen

The people of Ireland have voted yes for everyone
They accepted into words what was not spoken
They acknowledged men and women who are Irish and gay

We cast a vote for love
We changed the landscape
We made a space on this tiny isle of saints and scholars
For the world

My mother, Sue, died in her ninety-fifth year on Thursday, 28 May 2015. Over the next two days we brought her body to the Church of the Holy Rosary in Castlebar, and thence to the Old Cemetery, where she was buried with my father. Her favourite drive was across to Old Head at Clew Bay on the slopes of Croagh Patrick. She regularly visited Knock Shrine, where Our Lady is said to have appeared in 1879, wearing a white cloak and a crown of gold. The apparition was seen by fifteen people, who prayed the rosary in the rain. The Crowbar Brigades were thugs hired by the local landlord, Lord Lucan, during the famine of 1846/7. They cleared his land of tenants who were unable to pay the rent by dismantling their homes.

A Chaplet of Roses

Beneath the shadow of Croagh Patrick
In a lapping sea of lace
Head raised eyes closed
You gently floated away from shore
Towards the hope of the rising sun

A shaft of sunlight laid emphasis
On the structure of your sunken face
Presenting tight against the sufferings of old age

Your effigy infused an ordinary morning
With all the rainbow colours of a mother's love
In an extraordinary daily miracle

I understood that you were favoured
I knew you were ordained a saint

Weighed down with giving
I watched until you sank
The blast hit before the absent surface calmed
And then I turned and faced the land

Stripped of a welcome
No resting place left
With nobody to tell
The crowbar brigade has brought death to a sound foundation
A momentary fearful glimpse of what this clearance means

I have lost someone
Who loved me
Unconditionally

At Old Head where we'd look at the sea
I lit a beacon by the shoreline
A signal fire to show my love
For the young woman who became my mother

An eternal flame to prove my gratitude
For creating me in your image
For gifting me yourself
For as long as you drew breath

Thankfulness for setting me free
To appreciate our differences
My ambivalence
I'm aware you managed that well

Able to be proud declaring
You are my mother
I am your son
We have cared for each other
During two overlapping life-times
And now I am without

I pray that the alchemy of fire
May burn off the dross in our relationship
A purgatory of my own making
Since you never burdened me with expectations

The embers glow with the love you have nurtured
May the light guide your pilgrim's journey home

Refracted and reflected in the sea spray
You came to me across the foam
Wearing a white cloak and a coronet of golden roses
You didn't speak but held me in your gaze
As once you cradled your first-born in the curve of an arm
I stood in the rain reciting a decade of the rosary
With the beads you gave that my father owned

The tide on the turn shovelled up the sand
And you were gone from me
For ever

At my feet
A chaplet of roses
Floating gently on the ebb

Thank you
For your legacy
Of love

www.michaelmurphyauthor.com

IF YOU HAVE ENJOYED READING this book of poetry, then please tell others about it, and recommend *A Chaplet of Roses* to your friends.

And if you'd like to let me know how my poems have affected you, you can email me at info@michaelmurphyauthor.com. I'd welcome receiving your comments.

The website gives background information on *A Chaplet of Roses*. It also gives the latest news about book-signings, readings, and performances of my show, *Stories, Poetry and Dreams*. There's a section dealing with the first poetry collection, *The Republic of Love*, and two works of prose: *At Five in the Afternoon* and its sequel *The House of Pure Being*. The final part of that trilogy, *Lemons and the Waning Moon*, will be published in 2016.

Thank you for taking the time to read my poems. I hope they will continue to reward your attention.

Go dté tu slán!